SPANISH 1
LIFEPAC SI⌐

MW00720819

CONTENTS

Author: **Vicki Seeley Milunich, B.A., M.S. Ed.**
Editor: Alan Christopherson, M.S.
Graphic Design: Kyle Bennett, Jennifer Davis,
                     Alpha Omega Staff

Alpha Omega Publications

Published by Alpha Omega Publications, Inc.
300 North McKemy Avenue, Chandler, Arizona 85226-2618

SPANISH 1: LIFEPAC SIX
IN THE RESTAURANT

OBJECTIVES

When you have completed this LIFEPAC, you should be able to:

1. Use vocabulary related to food and parts of the body.

2. Use a variety of idiomatic phrases.

3. Conjugate a variety of verbs with irregular forms.

4. Express that something hurts.

5. Use **hay**.

6. Express numbers from 100–1,000,000.

7. Be aware of the South American countries where Spanish is spoken.

I. VOCABULARY & CONVERSATION PRACTICE

Conversación – En el restaurante

Pablo:	¿Qué quieres tomar?
Anita:	No sé. ¿Qué piensas en tomar?
Pablo:	Me gusta el arroz con pollo pero el biftec parece bien.
Anita:	El biftec aquí es muy delicioso pero prefiero el jamón con papas y una ensalada de verduras.
Pablo:	Parece bien. Miro la paella también.
Anita:	Tienes que decidir. Aquí viene el camarero.
El camarero:	Buenas noches. ¿En qué puedo servirles?
Pablo:	¿Qué es la especialidad del día?
El camarero:	Hoy tenemos la paella valenciana y una ensalada, o la menestra de ternera.
Pablo:	Los dos parecen deliciosas. Me gustaría la menestra de ternera. También una ensalada de verduras.
El camarero:	Está bien. ¿Y Ud.?
Anita:	Me gustaría la paella. Parece bien hoy.
El camarero:	¿Te gustaría una ensalada?
Anita:	Sí, por favor.
El camarero:	¿Y para beber?
Anita:	Me gustaría agua.
Pablo:	Lo mismo para mí.

Pablo, Anita and El camero

Translation – In the restaurant

Paul:	What do you want to have?
Anita:	I don't know. What are you thinking of having?
Paul:	I like the chicken and rice, but the steak seems good.
Anita:	The steak here is very delicious, but I prefer the ham and potatoes and a green salad.
Paul:	It seems (sounds) good. I'm looking at the paella also.
Anita:	You have to decide. Here comes the waiter.
Waiter:	Good evening. How may I help you?
Paul:	What is the specialty of the day?
Waiter:	Today we have the paella Valenciana and the veal stew.
Paul:	Both sound delicious. I would like the veal stew. Also a green salad.
Waiter:	Fine. And you?
Anita:	I would like the paella. It sounds good today.
Waiter:	Would you like a salad?
Anita:	Yes, please.
Waiter:	And to drink?
Anita:	I would like water.
Pablo:	The same for me.

Look at the conversation and write the meanings of the following words or phrases.

1.1

a. el arroz con pollo _____

b. el biftec _____

c. el jamón _____

d. papas _____

e. una ensalada de verduras _____

f. parece bien _____

g. la paella _____

h. el camarero _____

i. ¿En qué puedo servirles? _____

j. la especialidad del día _____

k. la menestra de ternera _____

l. lo mismo para mí _____

Conversación

1.2   Practice this conversation with your learning partner so that you may say it without looking at the text.

✔ Adult check _____

                        Initial   Date

3

El vocabulario de la comida – Food vocabulary

Las comidas – food:

la carne	meat
la carne asada	roast beef
el pollo	chicken
el pescado	fish
las chuletas de cerdo	pork chops
el biftec	steak
la ternera	veal
el jamón	ham
la hamburguesa	hamburger
el tocino	bacon

Los legumbres or las verduras – vegetables:

los frijoles	beans
las papas	potatoes
las zanahorias	carrots
las habichuelas	green beans
el maíz	corn
las espinacas	spinach
los guisantes	peas
la lechuga	lettuce
el tomate	tomato

Las frutas – fruits:

la manzana	apple
las uvas	grapes
las fresas	strawberries
la pera	pear
la naranja	orange
el melón	melon
el melocotón	peach
la piña	pineapple
el plátano	banana

Los postres – desserts:

los pasteles	pastries
las tartas	pies
el helado	ice cream
el pastel	cake
el flan	carmel custard

Las bebidas – drinks:

el agua	water
la leche	milk
el jugo	juice
el refresco	soft drink
el café	coffee
el té	tea
el chocolate	hot chocolate
el batido	shake

Otras comidas – other foods:

la sal	salt
la pimienta	pepper
el azúcar	sugar
la mantequilla	butter
el pan	bread
la mermelada	jam
la sopa	soup
las papas fritas	French fries
el cereal	cereal
los huevos	eggs
un sandwich	a sandwich
el yogur	yogurt
el arroz	rice
la pizza	pizza
la pasta	pasta

Verbs:

comer	to eat
tomar	to have as in food or drink, to take
beber	to drink
preparar	to prepare
cocinar	to cook
pedir	to order
poner la mesa	to set the table

El desayuno

El almuerzo

La cena

La merienda

 Complete the following statements using food vocabulary.

1.3

a. Para el desayuno, prefiero comer: _____

b. Para el almuerzo, prefiero comer: _____

c. Para la cena, prefiero comer: _____

d. Con la cena, prefiero beber: _____

e. Con el desayuno, prefiero beber: _____

f. Después de la escuela, tomo una merienda de: _____

g. Cuando tengo mucha hambre, tomo: _____

h. De postre, me gusta mucho: _____

i. Mi comida favorita es: _____

j. Me gusta preparar: _____

The verb **tomar** is used to express the concept of having food, although its other meaning is "to take." It does not mean to have, as in "I have five brothers." **Tener** is the common word used to express all other senses of having.

Some common restaurant expressions are:

¿En qué puedo servirles?	How may I help you?
¿Algo más?	Something else?
¿Qué les puedo traer?	What can I bring you?
¿Qué vas a pedir?	What are you going to order?
¿Quieres compartir?	Do you want to share?
¡Buen provecho!	Enjoy your meal.
Tengo mucha hambre.	I am very hungry
Tengo sed.	I am thirsty
La cuenta.	The check

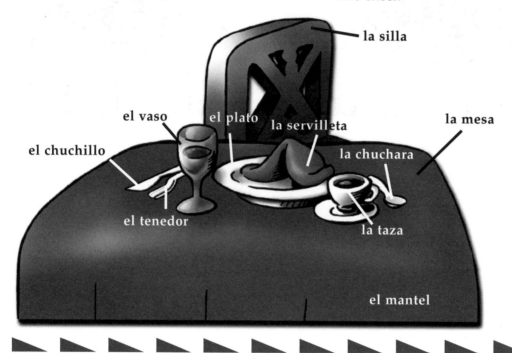

1.4 **Label the pictures.**

a. _____

_____

b. _____

_____

c. _____

_____

d. _____

e. _____

Conversación – Te toca a ti – It's your turn.

> **Complete these conversations.**

1.5   You and a friend are looking over the menu. Your friend makes certain statements. You prepare your responses to make a complete conversation.

Amigo/a: Me gusta este restaurante.

Tú:

Amigo/a: Pienso que voy a tomar el arroz con pollo. ¿Y tú?

Tú:

Amigo/a: No sé si quiero agua fría o un refresco.

Tú:

Amigo/a: Esta comida es excelente. ¿Quieres postre?

Tú:

Amigo/a: Me gustaría una fruta con queso.

Tú:

✔ Adult check _____
                          Initial   Date

1.6   You are the waiter in a restaurant and a gentleman comes in to eat.

El hombre: Buenas noches.

Tú:

El hombre: ¿Cuáles son las especialidades para hoy?

Tú:

El hombre: Me gustaría la menestra de ternera y una ensalada.

Tú:

El hombre: Agua fría ahora y el café con el postre.

Tú:

El hombre: Pienso que quiero una tarta de manzana con el café.

✔ Adult check _____
                          Initial   Date

SELF TEST 1

1.01   **After each word write** D **for desayuno,** A **for almuerzo,** C **for cena, or** M **for merienda. Some problems may have more than one answer.** (3 pts. each)

1. los huevos   _____

2. las papas   _____

3. el helado   _____

4. el biftec   _____

5. el tocino   _____

6. el batido   _____

7. la naranja   _____

8. las espinicas   _____

9. un sandwich   _____

10. el pastel   _____

1.02   **After each word write** C **for carne,** B **for bebida,** F **for fruta, or** L **for legumbre.** (3 pts. each)

1. los guisantes   _____

2. el jamón   _____

3. el té   _____

4. las fresas   _____

5. el pollo   _____

6. el jugo   _____

7. la piña   _____

8. las zanahorias   _____

9. los frijoles   _____

10. la manzana   _____

1.03 **Answer the following questions in complete sentences.** (3 pts. each)

    a. ¿Qué vas a pedir?

    b. ¿Quieres tomar el almuerzo?

    c. ¿Quieres algo a beber?

    d. ¿Qué tipo de carne prefieres?

    e. Cuándo tienes mucha sed, ¿qué prefieres tomar?

    f. ¿Qué te gusta comer para el desayuno?

    g. ¿Qué le gusta a tu familia para la cena?

    h. Después de correr mucho, ¿qué prefieres?

    i. Cuándo tienes frío, ¿qué vas a comer?

    j. Para la merienda, ¿qué comes?

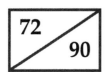

72 / 90

Score _____

Teacher check _____
                             Initial   Date

II. IRREGULAR VERBS

Conversación – Después de comer

Luis:	Ana, vamos a dar un paseo por el parque.
Ana:	¡Qué buena idea! Necesito caminar.
Luis:	Siempre como demasiado cuando comemos en el Café Marcos.
Ana:	Yo también. Doy las gracias que no comemos allí a menudo.
Luis:	Pienso que veo a Miguel y Diana allá.
Ana:	Tienes razón. Vamos a hablar con ellos.
Luis:	¡Hola, Miguel y Diana! ¿Cómo están?
Miguel:	Bien, gracias. ¿Y ustedes?
Ana:	Bien. ¿Qué hacen?
Diana:	Damos un paseo y admiramos como los bancos nuevos dan al fuente.
Luis:	Vamos a sentarnos en uno de los bancos.
Miguel:	A los niños les gusta jugar con el agua en el fuente. Son cómicos con los pequeños barcos.
Ana:	¡Qué mono!

Translation – After eating

Luis:	Ann, let's take a walk through the park.
Ann:	What a good idea! I need to walk.
Luis:	I always eat too much when we eat at the Café Marcos.
Ann:	Me too. I am thankful that we don't eat there often.
Luis:	I think that I see Mike and Diane over there.
Ann:	You're right. Let's go talk with them
Luis:	Hi, Mike and Diane. How are you?
Mike:	Fine, thanks. And you?
Ann:	Good. What are you doing?
Diane:	We are taking a walk and admiring how the new benches face the fountain.
Luis:	Let's sit on one of the benches.
Mike:	The children like to play with the water in the fountain. They are comical with the small boats.
Ann:	How cute!

Look at the two conversations and translate the following expressions.

2.1   a. dar un paseo _____

b. por _____

c. ¡Qué buena idea! _____

d. demasiado_____

e. doy las gracias _____

f. a menudo _____

g. allá _____

h. los bancos _____

i. el fuente _____

j. sentarnos _____

k. barcos _____

l. ¡Qué mono! _____

The verb dar – to give

Dar is conjugated irregularly in the **yo** form.

yo	**doy**	nts.	**damos**
tú	**das**	vts.	**dais**
él	**da**	ellos	**dan**
ella	**da**	ellas	**dan**
Usted	**da**	Ustedes	**dan**

Dar is also used in many idioms:

dar las gracias	to thank, give thanks, be thankful
dar un paseo	to take a walk
dar a	to face

Fill in the blank with the correct form of the verb dar **and translate the sentence.**

2.2

a. Nts. _____ un paseo por el campo.

b. Yo _____ las gracias a mi abuela.

c. Ellos _____ los regalos a sus primos.

d. Tú _____ los papels al profesor.

e. El edificio _____ a la calle.

The verb ver – to see

Ver is also irregular in the **yo** form in that it retains the **e** before adding the **o**. All other forms are regular.

yo	**veo**	nts.	**vemos**
tú	**ves**	vts.	**veis**
él	**ve**	ellos	**ven**
ella	**ve**	ellas	**ven**
Usted	**ve**	Ustedes	**ven**

 Fill in the blank with the correct form of the verb ver **and then translate the sentences.**

2.3

1. Yo _____ a mi amigo, Jorge.

2. Ud. _____ las flores bonitas.

3. Tú _____ las fotos de Daniela.

4. Nts._____ a nuestros abuelos.

5. Alicia _____ el vestido rojo.

NOTE: Please be careful when working with the verb **ver**. The forms are very similar to the forms of **ir** and can easily be confused. **Ver** has the **e** in the forms while **ir** has the **a**.

Verbs like conocer

Conocer is the verb that goes to **conozco** in the **yo** form and retains normal conjugation throughout the rest of the forms. There are several other verbs which follow this same pattern. They are:

agradecer	to thank	**yo agradezco**
aparecer	to appear	**yo aparezco**
conducir	to drive, conduct	**yo conduzco**
desaparecer	to disappear	**yo desaparezco**
obedecer	to obey	**yo obedezco**
ofrecer	to offer	**yo ofrezco**
parecer	to seem, look like	**yo parezco**
producir	to produce	**yo produzco**
reconocer	to recognize	**yo reconozco**
traducir	to translate	**yo traduzco**

Fill in the blank with the correct form of one of the verbs from the list on the previous page. Be sure to choose the correct verb for the meaning of the sentence, then translate your sentence.

2.4

a. Mi padre _____ el coche.

b. Los estudiantes _____ las frases.

c. Mariana _____ enferma.

d. Nts. _____ a Dios cada día.

e. Yo _____ buen trabajo.

f. Tú _____ al Sr. Chavez de su foto.

g. Nts. _____ a nuestros padres.

h. Mi hermano _____ conducir al concierto.

i. Los niños _____ a mi puerta a las seis de la mañana.

j. Mi dinero siempre _____ rápidamente.

SELF TEST 2

2.01 **Fill in the blank with the correct form of the verb** ver. (5 pts. each)

a. Yo _____ al camarero.

b. Nts. _____ a nuestros amigos.

c. Tú _____ a Raúl.

d. José _____ la mesa desocupada.

e. Los jovenes _____ la película nueva.

2.02 **Fill in the blank with the correct form of the verb** dar. (5 pts. each)

a. Nts. _____ un paseo en el parque.

b. Yo _____ las gracias a mi abuela.

c. Tú _____ un regalo a Jorge.

d. El hotel _____ a la tienda.

e. Mis tíos _____ las bebidas a mis padres.

2.03 **Fill in the blank with the correct form of the verb in parentheses.** (5 pts. each)

a. Yo _____ a mis padres. (obedecer)

b. Nts. _____ el párafo. (traducir)

c. Tú _____ a José bien. (conocer)

d. El restaurante _____ comida excelente. (producir)

e. Ricardo _____ muy bien. (conducir)

2.04 **Answer the following questions in complete sentences.** (5 pts. each)

a. ¿Quién ofrece conducir a la fiesta?

b. ¿Cuál reconoces mejor?

c. ¿Qué traducen Uds.?

d. ¿Cómo parece Miguel hoy?

e. ¿A quién agradece Ud. cuando recibe algo simpático?

Score _____

Teacher check _____
Initial   Date

III. IDIOMS

Conversación – El cuerpo humano

David:	¡Ay, tengo un dolor de cabeza!
Arturo:	¿Por qué?
David:	Mi hermano toca la música muy fuerte.
Arturo:	¡Qué lástima! Vamos a ir al cine.
David:	No. No quiero andar. Tengo un dolor de pie.
Arturo:	¿Por qué?
David:	Mi hermanita corrió su bicicleta sobre mis pies.
Arturo:	¡Qué pena! Vamos a comer helado.
David:	No puedo porque tengo dolor de dientes cuando como algo frío.
Arturo:	¡Qué horrible!
David:	No sé qué hacer.
Arturo:	Vamos a mirar la televisión.
David:	Está bien. Vamos.

Translation – The human body

David:	Oh, I have a headache!
Arthur:	Why?
David:	My brother plays the music very loud.
Arthur:	What a pity! Let's go to the movies.
David:	No. I don't want to walk. I have a sore foot.
Arthur:	Why?
David:	My little sister ran her bike over my feet.
Arthur:	What a pain! Let's eat ice cream.
David:	I can't because my teeth ache when I eat something cold.
Arthur:	How horrible!
David:	I don't know what to do.
Arthur:	Let's watch television.
David:	Okay. Let's.

  Complete this activity.

3.1   Practice this conversation with your learning partner and present it to the class. Try to memorize as much as you can.

✔ Adult check _____

                                         Initial   Date

Look at the conversation on the previous page and translate the following words and phrases.

3.2   a. un dolor de cabeza _____

           b. muy fuerte _____

           c. ¡Qué lástima! _____

           d. un dolor de pie _____

           e. ¡Qué pena! _____

           f. dolor de dientes _____

           g. ¡Qué horrible! _____

El cuerpo humano

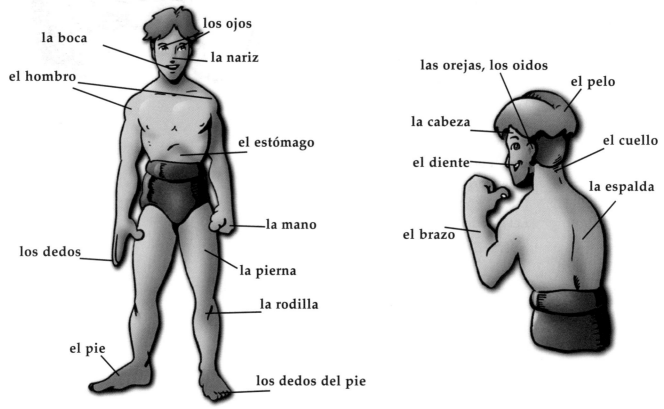

Answer the following questions using a body part(s).

3.3   a. ¿Qué está sobre la cabeza? _____

           b. ¿De qué tiene dos en la cabeza? _____

           c. ¿Qué parte se usa para hablar? _____

           d. ¿Qué se usa para dar un paseo? _____

e. ¿Qué es la parte entre la espalda y la cabeza? _____

f. ¿Adónde va la comida que come? _____

g. ¿Qué es la parte sobre el pie? _____

h. ¿Qué es la parte al fin del brazo? _____

i. ¿Dónde se encuentran los dedos? _____

j. ¿Qué es la parte pequeña de los pies? _____

To say that a person has an ache or a certain body part hurts, the expression **tener dolor de + the body part** is used. For example:

> **Tengo dolor de cabeza**   says   I have a headache.
>
> **Tienes dolor de brazo**   says   You have a sore arm *or* Your arm hurts.

Using this concept, translate what aches are described below. Be sure to remember the conjugation of tener.

yo tengo	nts. tenemos
tú tienes	vts. tenéis
él, ella, Ud. tiene	ellos, ellas, Uds. tienen.

3.4   a. Maria tiene dolor de pierna. _____

b. Uds. tienen dolor de pies. _____

c. Nts. tenemos dolor de estómago. _____

d. Yo tengo dolor de diente. _____

e. Tú tienes dolor de mano. _____

f. Hector tiene dolor de oreja. _____

g. Yo tengo dolor de dedo de pie. _____

h. Ud. tiene dolor de espalda. _____

i. Tú tienes dolor de cuello. _____

j. Nts. tenemos dolor de hombros. _____

Write under the picture which body part is missing.

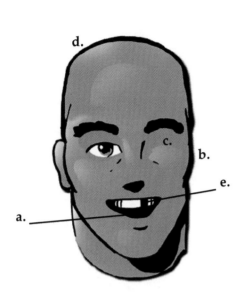

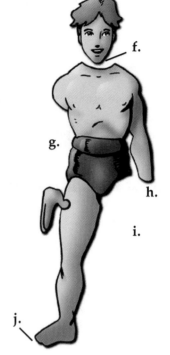

3.5

a. _____   f. _____

b. _____   g. _____

c. _____   h. _____

d. _____   i. _____

e. _____   j. _____

Another way to say that some part of the body hurts is to use the verb **doler**. This "shoe" verb also works like **gustar**. For example:

Me **duele** la cabeza.	My head hurts. (Literally, The head hurts me.)
Me **duelen** los pies.	My feet hurt. (Literally, The feet hurt me.)
Te **duele** la pierna.	My leg hurts.
Te **duelen** los brazos.	My arms hurt.
Le **duele** el cuello.	His/her/your neck hurts.
Le **duelen** las oídos.	His/her/your [inner] ears hurt.
Nos **duele** la espalda.	Our back hurts.
Nos **duelen** los ojos.	Our eyes hurt.
Les **duele** el estómago.	Their/your stomach hurts.
Les **duelen** las manos.	Their/your hands hurt.

Remember when one part hurts to use **duele** and for more than one part use **duelen**.

18

Fill in the blank with the correct form, duele **or** duelen. **Then translate the sentence.**

3.6

a. Me _____ el dedo.

b. Nos _____ los pies.

c. Les _____ las espaldas.

d. Te _____ los ojos.

e. Le _____ la cabeza.

SELF TEST 3

3.01   **Write the word for each lettered item.** (5 pts. each)

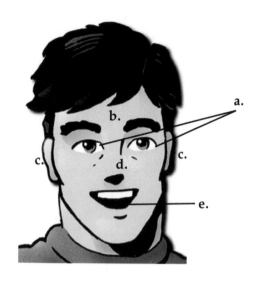
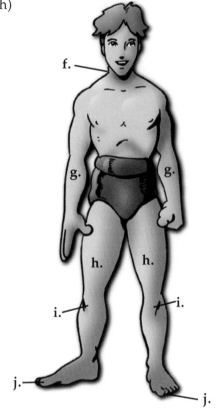

a. _____   f. _____

b. _____   g. _____

c. _____   h. _____

d. _____   i. _____

e. _____   j. _____

3.02   **Translate to Spanish two ways, using** tener dolor de **and** doler. (8 pts. each)

a. My feet hurt._____

b. His leg hurts. _____

c. Our heads hurt._____

d. Your (fam. sing.) ear hurts. _____

e. Their arms hurt. _____

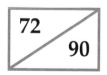

Score   _____

Teacher check _____
                         Initial   Date

20

IV. *HAY*

Conversación – Un viaje a Sudamérica

Sr. Gomez:	Mi familia y yo vamos a hacer un viaje por Sudamérica.
Sr. Lopez:	¿Adónde vas?
Sr. Gomez:	Vamos a Argentina, Uruguay, Paraguay y finalmente Bolivia.
Sr. Lopez:	Parece un viaje magnífico.
Sr. Gomez:	Pienso que sí.
Sr. Lopez:	Haga Ud. el favor de mandar unas tarjetas postales a mi familia.
Sr. Gomez:	Por supuesto. Vamos a ver muchos sitios interesantes.
Sr. Lopez:	¿Cuáles son?
Sr. Gomez:	En Argentina, vamos a ver el Cristo de los Andes. Y cerca de las fronteras de Argentina, y Uruguay vamos a ver las cataratas de Iguázu. En Bolivia, vamos a visitar la ciudad capital de La Paz. Y hay muchos más lugares que queremos ver.
Sr. Lopez:	Va a ser un viaje inolvidable.
Sr. Gomez:	Espero que sí.

Translation – A trip to South America

Mr. Gomez:	My family and I are taking a trip through South America.
Mr. Lopez:	Where are you going?
Mr. Gomez:	We are going to Argentina, Uruguay, Paraguay and finally, Bolivia.
Mr. Lopez:	It seems like a magnificient trip.
Mr. Gomez:	I think so.
Mr. Lopez:	Please send some postcards to my family.
Mr. Gomez:	Of course. We are going to see many interesting places.
Mr. Lopez:	What are they?
Mr. Gomez:	In Argentina we are going to see Christ of the Andes. And near the borders of Argentina and Uruguay we are going to see the Iguazu Waterfalls. In Bolivia, we are going to visit the capital city of La Paz. And there are more places we want to see.
Mr. Lopez:	It is going to be an unforgettable trip.
Mr. Gomez:	I hope so.

Look at the two translations of the conversation and write the meaning of the following.

4.1
a. vamos a _____

b. hacer un viaje _____

c. por _____

d. finalmente _____

d. parece _____

f. pienso que sí _____

g. haga Ud. el favor de _____

h. tarjetas postales _____

i. sitios _____

j. las fronteras _____

k. las cataratas _____

l. hay _____

m. lugares _____

n. inolvidable _____

o. espero que sí _____

Idioms using hacer

Idioms are those phrases and expressions that, when literally translated, do not make sense exactly. For example, in English when we say, "It is raining cats and dogs," do we really mean that there are cats and dogs falling from the sky? No, it simply means that it is pouring very hard. Think about the following "idioms." Do they really mean what they say?

> He's got a green thumb.
> She's as sharp as a tack.
> They're looking at the world through rose-colored glasses.
> He's fast as lightning.

There are many idioms in Spanish. In this lesson we will discuss four that use the verb **hacer**. **Hacer** normally means "to make or do." But in the following they do not translate that way when we go from "good" Spanish to "good" English. Remember the conjugations of **hacer** are: **hago, haces, hace, hacemos, hacéis, hacen.**

22

Hacer una pregunta means "to ask a question." If it were translated literally, it would mean "to make or do a question."

Hacer un viaje means "to take a trip." Literally translated, it means "to make or do a trip."

Hacer la maleta means "to pack a suitcase." Literally it means "to make or do a suitcase."

Haga Ud. el favor de + an infinitive means "please." Literally it means "do the favor of."

Haga is a form of the verb **hacer** in the command/subjunctive tenses.

 Read the following paragraph and answer the questions that follow.

La madre de Anita hace las maletas para la famila. Hacen un viaje a la playa. Anita está muy emocionante. Le gusta ir a la playa. Siempre hace muchas preguntas de su madre como "¿Cuándo vamos a la playa?", "¿Puedo tomar mis juguetes de arena?", "¿Puedo nadar en el océano?" La madre de Anita hace una pregunta de Anita, "¿Haga el favor de no hace muchas preguntas? Estoy muy ocupada." Entonces, Anita va a su cuarto para la ropa que va a necesitar para el viaje. La madre está muy contenta que Anita va a ayudar.

4.2

    a. ¿Qué hace la madre de Anita?

    b. ¿Por qué?

    c. ¿Qué hace Anita?

    d. ¿Cuántas preguntas hace?

    e. ¿Por qué la madre no quiere las preguntas?

    f. ¿Qué decide hacer Anita?

    g. ¿Por qué la madre de Anita está contenta?

Conversation Practice

> Complete this conversation. Be careful to look at the response given after yours to make sure the conversational flow is maintained.

4.3   Teresa: ¿Vas de vacacciones?

Tú: _____

Teresa: Me gustaría viajar allí.

Tú: _____

Teresa: ¿Cuántos días vas a estar allí?

Tú: _____

Teresa: Pienso que tienen comida excelente en los restaurantes.

Tú: _____

Teresa: Prefiero probar la comida nueva como paella or menestra.

Tú: _____

Teresa: ¿Qué sitios quieres ver?

Tú: _____

Teresa: Me gusta caminar por los museos y los parques. Me gusta observar al arte y a la gente.

Tú: _____

Teresa: ¡Buen viaje!

Tú: _____

✔ Adult check _____

                              Initial   Date

SPANISH

ONE

LIFEPAC 6
TEST

78 / 98

Name _____

Date _____

Score _____

LIFEPAC TEST

1. Label the following pictures in Spanish. (2 pts. each)

a.

b.

c.

d.

e.

f.

g.

h.

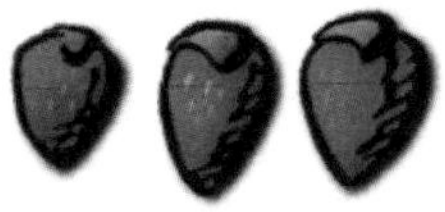

i.

j.

k.

l.

m.

n.

o.

a. _____

b. _____

c. _____

d. _____

e. _____

f. _____

g. _____

h. _____

i. _____

j. _____

k. _____

l. _____

m. _____

n. _____

o. _____

2.   Label the parts of the person's body. (2 pts. each)

a. _____

b. _____

c. _____

d. _____

e. _____

f. _____

g. _____

h. _____

i. _____

j. _____

k. _____

3.   Write out the following numbers. (2 pts. each)

a. 457 _____

b. 3,821 _____

c. 93,649 _____

d. 6,734,573 _____

_____

e. 356 _____

4.   Fill in the blank with the correct form of the verb in parentheses. (2 pts. each)

a. Mario_____ la pregunta. (hacer)

b. Tú _____ las gracias. (dar)

c. Yo _____ a mis amigos. (ver)

d. Nts._____ un paseo. (dar)

e. Ellos_____ la tarea. (traducir)

f. Uds. _____ dolor de cabeza. (tener)

g. La iglesia _____ al supermercado. (dar)

h. Yo _____ un viaje a España. (hacer)

i. Yo _____ buen trabajo. (producir)

j. Nts._____ al profesor. (conocer)

5. Answer the following questions in complete Spanish sentences. (2 pts. each)

a. ¿Dónde te duele?

b. ¿Cuánto cuesta un coche nuevo?

c. ¿Quién conoce a Luis?

d. ¿Adónde dan Uds. un paseo?

e. ¿Qué tomas para el desayuno?

6. List five South American countries and state one fact about each. (2 pts. each)

a.

b.

c.

d.

e.

Other Idioms

echar de menos – to miss

Echo de menos a mis amigos.
(I miss my friends.)

echar una carta al correo – to mail a letter

Echa una carta al correo a su abuela.
(He is mailing a letter to his grandmother.)

creer que sí (no) – to think so (not)

Creemos que sí.
(We think so.)

estar de pie – to be standing

Están de pie en cola para los billetes.
(They are standing in line for the tickets.)

querer decir – to mean

Quiere decir que no puede ir.
(He means that he can't go.)

salir bien (mal) – to come out well (badly), to pass (fail)

Salgo bien en el examen de historia.
(I did well on the history test.)
**El viaje a Madrid sale mal
desafortunadamente.**
(The trip to Madrid is coming out badly,
  unfortunately.)

Fill in the blank with one of the idioms above so that the sentence makes sense.

4.4

a. ¿Qué _____ "la habichuela" en inglés?

b. ¿Vas a visitar a España? _____

c. Tengo que_____ a mi amiga en La Argentina.

d. Los estudiantes _____ en el examen de inglés.

e. Tenemos que_____ para ver el juego.

f. Durante el viaje vas a_____ a tu familia.

g. Mi dinero siempre_____ rápidamente.

Conversation Practice

Complete this conversation. Be careful to look at the response given after yours to make sure the conversational flow is maintained.

4.5   Luis: ¿Vas de vacaciones a Bolivia?

Tú: _____

Luis: ¿Qué quiere decir? ¿No vas a Bolivia?

Tú: _____

Luis: ¿Vas a echar de menos a tu amiga?

Tú: _____

Luis: Puedes echar una carta al correo.

Tú: _____

Luis: Todo va a salir bien.

Tú: _____

✔ Adult check _____
                          Initial   Date

26

SELF TEST 4

4.01   **Vocabulary matching.** (2 pts. each)

_____ 1. echar de menos   a. to pack a suitcase

_____ 2. hacer una pregunta   b. to mail a letter

_____ 3. salir bien   c. please

_____ 4. querer decir   d. to be standing

_____ 5. hacer una maleta   e. to think so

_____ 6. estar de pie   f. to ask a question

_____ 7. haga Ud. el favor de   g. to take a trip

_____ 8. creer que sí   h. to miss

_____ 9. echar una carta al correo   i. to mean

_____ 10. hacer un viaje   j. to come out well

4.02   **Answer the following questions in complete Spanish sentences.** (8 pts. each)

a. ¿Qué quiere decir "hola" en inglés?

b. ¿Adónde hace Ud. un viaje?

c. ¿Dónde está de pie?

d. ¿A quién echan Uds. una carta al correo?

e. ¿A qué sale bien Luis?

f. ¿A quien echa de menos Lara?

g. ¿Cuándo necesita hacer una maleta?

h. ¿Por qué hace preguntas?

i. ¿Crees que Manuel va a estar aquí?

j. Haga Ud. el favor de escribir su nombre.

80 / 100	Score _____
	Teacher check _____
	Initial Date

V. REVIEW EXERCISES, NUMBERS 100–1,000,000

Conversación – ¿Cuánto?

Enrique, un chico de tres años hace muchas preguntas de su padre.

Enrique:	¿Cuántas pies en una milla?
Padre:	Cinco mil doscientos ochenta pies.
Enrique:	¿Cuántos pies en un campo de fútbol americano?
Padre:	Trescientos.
Enrique:	¿Cuántas personas hay en nuestra ciudad?
Padre:	Hay cincuenta mil personas.
Enrique:	¿Cuánto cuesta nuestro coche nuevo?
Padre:	Cuesta veinte mil dólares.
Enrique:	¿Cuántas estrellas hay en el cielo?
Padre:	Hay millones de estrellas.
Enrique:	¿Cuántas libras hay en una tonelada?
Padre:	Hay dos mil. ¿Por qué hace tantas preguntas?
Enrique:	No sé.

Translation – How much?

Enrique, a three-year-old boy, asks his father many questions.

Enrique:	How many feet in a mile?
Father:	Five thousand, two hundred and eighty feet.
Enrique:	How many feet in a football field?
Father:	Three hundred.
Enrique:	How many people are there in our city?
Father:	There are fifty thousand people.
Enrique:	How much does our new car cost?
Father:	It costs twenty thousand dollars.
Enrique:	How many stars are there in the sky?
Father:	There are millions of stars.
Enrique:	How many pounds in a ton?
Father:	There are two thousand. Why are you asking so many questions?
Enrique:	I don't know.

Look at the conversation and give the meaning for the following phrases or words.

5.1   a. pies _____

b. una mila _____

c. cinco mil doscientos _____

d. un campo _____

e. trescientos _____

f. cincuenta mil _____

g. cuesta _____

h. veinte mil _____

i. estrellas _____

j. el cielo _____

k. millones _____

l. libras _____

m. una tonelada _____

n. dos mil _____

o. tantas _____

Numbers

100 – 900			
100	**ciento** (cien)	600	**seiscientos**/as
200	**doscientos**/as	700	**setecientos**/as*
300	**trescientos**/as	800	**ochocientos**/as
400	**cuatrocientos**/as	900	**novecientos**/as*
500	**quinientos**/as*		

*Note that 500, 700 and 900 do not follow the pattern of the others. Please take time to examine the spelling of these three numbers.

1,000 – 100,000,000			
1,000	**mil**	1,000,000	**millón** (de)
5,000	**cinco mil**	5,000,000	**cinco millones** (de)
100,000	**cien mil**	100,000,000	**cien millones** (de)

29

Notes:

1. **Y** is used only between the numbers 16–99.

        234 doscientos treinta y cuatro

        368 tres mil seiscientos ochenta y cinco

2. **Uno** and **ciento** are the only numbers that will agree with the nouns they modify.

Una casa	one (a) house
setecientos coches	seven hundred cars
mil personas	a thousand people
cincuenta dolares	fifty dollars

3. **Ciento** is also shortened to **cien** when used before a noun.

cien días	one hundred days	**cien ideas**	one hundred ideas
cien gatos	one hundred cats	**cien libras**	one hundred pounds

4. **Un** is never used with **ciento** or **mil**. But **un** must be used with **millón**. **Millón** also requires **de** before the noun.

ciento setenta	one hundred seventy
mil	one thousand
dos millones de años	two million years
cinco millones de dolares	five millon dollars

 Write out the following numbers.

5.2   a. 6,830 _____

       b. 1,003,752 _____

       c. 24,961 _____

       d. 987 _____

       e. 7,463 _____

       f. 352,671,538 _____

       g. 785,073 _____

       h. 333,444 _____

       i. 23,495 _____

       j. 975,246 _____

Conversation Practice

> **Complete this conversation. Be careful to look at the response given after yours to make sure the conversational flow is maintained.**

5.3   Paco: ¿Qué año es el coche de tu padre?

         Tú: _____

         Paco: Mi padre tiene un coche de mil novecientos cincuenta y cinco.

         Tú: _____

         Paco: Es rojo y va muy rápidamente.

         Tú: _____

         Paco: Mi tío tiene un coche de mil novecientos setenta y tres que es bello.

         Tú: _____

         Paco: Ellos van a los espectáculos de coches en el verano.

         Tú: _____

         Paco: Me gusta ir con ellos.

      ✔ Adult check _____

                                     Initial   Date

> **Write out the following expressions using the correct form of** ciento.

5.4   a. 100 friends _____

        b. 190 _____

        c. 400 houses_____

        d. 500 persons_____

        e. 100 ideas _____

Write out the following expressions.

5.5   a. a million stars _____

        b. 3 million years _____

        c. one thousand days _____

        d. eighty weeks _____

        e. 45 hours _____

SELF TEST 5

5.01   **Write out the following numbers.** (10 pts. each)

   a. 5,682 _____

   b. 89,531 _____

   c. 104,495 _____

   d. 4,375,934 _____

   e. 73,208 _____

5.02   **Write out the following expressions.** (10 pts. each)

   a. 1,000 days _____

   b. a million places _____

   c. $500.00 _____

   d. 100 hours _____

   e. 397 _____

<table>
<tr><td>80 / 100</td></tr>
</table>

Score _____

Teacher check _____
                        Initial   Date

33

VI. THE GEOGRAPHY OF SOUTH AMERICA

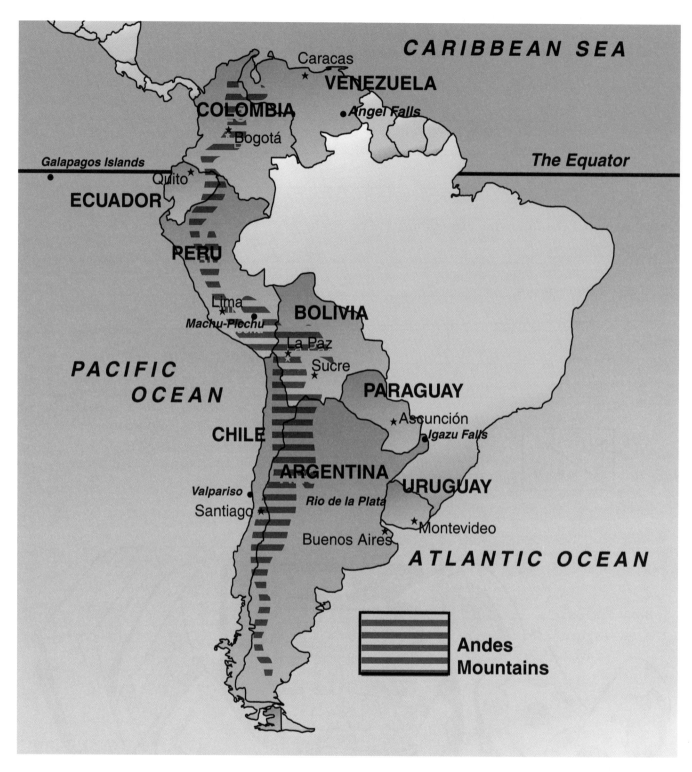

South America is a continent of nine Spanish speaking countries and four non-Spanish speaking countries. It is a continent of vast geographical variety. Along the western regions extending from the Colombian/Venezuelan border to the southern most part of Chile are the Andes Mountains. This mountain range contains volcanoes, high peaks and a lost city. There are also areas of plains known as the Pampas in Colombia, Venezuela and Argentina. In the northern region of Chile is a desert. Since the majority of South America lies south of the equator in the southern hemisphere, the seasons are the reverse of ours.

Venezuela is the richest oil-producing country in South America. Its capital is **Caracas**. It is bordered by the Caribbean Sea to the north, Guyana to the east, Brazil to the south and Colombia to the west. It is approximately 1.3 times the size of Texas. The majority of the population is Mestizo followed by White, Black and Indian. Their independence was claimed on July 5, 1821. Venezuela boasts the highest waterfalls in South America, aptly named Angel Falls. Venezuela has areas of buffalo herds. The Araya region is known for its salt flats. The Paraguana Peninsula is one area which is extremely arid. The Zula region is the main oil-producing region.

Colombia is another oil-producing country. It shares frontiers with Venezuela, Brazil, Peru, Ecuador, Panama. Its aqueous borders include the Pacific Ocean, the Atlantic Ocean and the Caribbean Sea. Its capital is **Bogotá** which has a population of over five million. The ethnic makeup of the country's population is Mestizo, White, Mulatto and Black. The government is a republic and became independent from Spain in 1810. The country has three main geographical regions. The mountainous area along the Pacific Ocean is called the Andean region and is where the Andes Mountains begin. The Atlantic Ocean/Caribbean Sea region is called the Caribbean region and boasts many beautiful beaches. The third region borders Peru and Brazil. This is the Amazón region which is generally covered by lush tropical jungle called the "selva."

Ecuador is a small Spanish speaking country in South America. It is bordered by Colombia, Peru and the Pacific Ocean. Its capital is **Quito** (the only capital in the world to begin with the letter Q) with a population of more than a million people. Its ethnic make up is Mestizo, Indian, Spanish and Black. This republic became independent in 1822. This country is one of the largest exporters of bananas. It also exports petroleum, cocoa, coffee and shrimp. The Galapagos Islands are located 600 miles west off the coast of Ecuador. These islands are home to huge tortoises and other unique animals.

Peru is located on the western coast of South America. It shares frontiers with Ecuador, Brazil, Colombia, Bolivia, Chile and the Pacific Ocean. Its capital is **Lima** with a population of more than six million. This country enjoys a variety of ethnic backgrounds—Indian, Mestizo, White, Black, Japanese and Chinese. Its government is a republic, having gained independence from Spain in 1821. Coffee, sugar, cotton and coffee are major exports. This country was part of the most powerful Inca empire. The Incas were known for their skills in architecture, engineering, textiles and social organizations. The Andes Mountains cover the majority of this country. High in these mountains is the famous Inca ruins of the city of Machu-Picchu. The oldest university in South America, the University of San Marcos, is located in Lima.

Bolivia is one of two landlocked nations in South America. It shares borders with Peru, Brazil, Paraguay, Argentina and Chile. Bolivia has the unique distinction of being the only country in South America to have two capitals. Its administrative capital is **La Paz**. Its judicial and legal capital is **Sucre**. The ethnic background of this country is primarily Indian—Quechua and Aymara—as well as mixed and European. Bolivia is rich in minerals, coffee, soybeans and sugar. Lake Titicaca is the highest navigable lake in the world. It is located on the border between Bolivia and Peru.

Chile is the narrowest and longest country in South America. It is nearly 4,000 miles long. It shares borders with Argentina, Peru, Bolivia and the Pacific Ocean. Its capital is **Santiago** with a population of nearly five million people. Valparaiso is Chile's largest port on the west coast of South America. Because of its tremendous length going north to south, Chile has a variety of geographical regions including desert, mountains, beaches, greenlands and almost arctic areas. Cristo de los Andes is a large statue of Christ located in the Andes Mountains between Chile and Argentina. It was built to honor the peaceful settlement of a boundary dispute between these two nations.

Paraguay is the other landlocked nation in South America. It is bordered by Argentina, Brazil and Bolivia. **Asunción** is the capital, having approximately a half a million inhabitants. The general makeup of the population is nearly 95% Mestizo, with the remaining five percent White and Indian. This country—along with Argentina, Urugauy and Chile—are in the South Temperate Zone which means that the seasons are the reverse of ours. Paraguay is the main producer of "yerba mate" which is a popular tea drunk widely throughout Paraguay and Argentina.

Uruguay is located on the eastern coast between Brazil and Argentina. Its capital is **Montevideo** with a population of nearly 1.2 million. The ethnic makeup of this country varies from the previously mentioned countries. Its population is 88% White, mainly of European descent, with the remaining 12% Mestizo and Black. This country is the smallest of the Spanish speaking countries of South America.

Argentina is located south and west of Uruguay. It is the largest of the Spanish speaking countries on this continent. Its capital is **Buenos Aires** with a population of more than 13 million people. The ethnic diversity here comes from the "melting pot" of Europeans that settled here between 1850 and the present. Thus a variety of languages may be heard besides Spanish—Italian, German, French and English. The Rio de la Plata is the river area dividing Argentina from Uruguay. Iguazú Falls are located between Argentina and Brazil. They are higher than Niagara Falls in New York.

 Complete the following activity.

6.1   Look at the map and label the countries and their capitals.

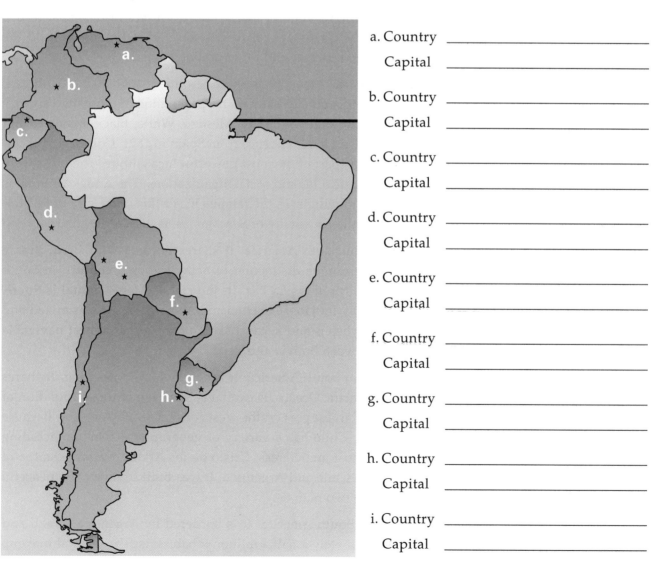

a. Country _____

   Capital _____

b. Country _____

   Capital _____

c. Country _____

   Capital _____

d. Country _____

   Capital _____

e. Country _____

   Capital _____

f. Country _____

   Capital _____

g. Country _____

   Capital _____

h. Country _____

   Capital _____

i. Country _____

   Capital _____

Match the countries with their descriptions. Answers may be used more than once.

6.2

_____ 1. The smallest country.

_____ 2. The largest country.

_____ 3. The country which produces the most oil.

_____ 4. The country with two capitals.

_____ 5. The narrowest country.

_____ 6. The country which is nearly completely in the Andes Mountains.

_____ 7. The Galapagos Islands are located 600 miles from this country's coastline.

_____ 8. This country has borders on both the Pacific and Atlantic Ocean.

_____ 9. These two countries are landlocked.

_____ 10. This country has waterfalls higher than Niagara Falls.

_____ 11. This country produces the tea called yerba mate.

_____ 12. This country has the highest waterfalls in South America.

_____ 13. This country was part of the Inca Empire.

_____ 14. This country boasts a desert and mountains.

_____ 15. This country is where the Andes Mountains begin.

_____ 16. Christ of the Andes is located in this country.

_____ 17. This country is divided into three main regions: Andean, Caribbean and Amazon.

_____ 18. This country is one of the largest exporters of bananas.

_____ 19. This country has the highest navigable lake in the world, Lake Titicaca.

_____ 20. These two countries are divided by the Rio de la Plata.

a. Argentina

b. Bolivia

c. Chile

d. Columbia

e. Ecuador

f. Paraguay

g. Peru

h. Uruguay

i. Venezuela

SELF TEST 6

6.01   **Identify each country and its capital(s) on the map below.** (4 pts. each answer)

a. Country _____

   Capital _____

b. Country _____

   Capital _____

c. Country _____

   Capital _____

d. Country _____

   Capital _____

e. Country _____

   Capital _____

f. Country _____

   Capital _____

g. Country _____

   Capital _____

h. Country _____

   Capital _____

i. Country _____

   Capital _____

6.02   **Identify the country by the description given.** (3 pts. each)

a. The largest country which has a "melting pot" population of European and Indian cultures. It is home of the Iguazú Falls.

b. This is the smallest country with a large population of White people.

c. The Andes Mountains begin in this country and it has borders on both the Atlantic and Pacific Ocean.

d. This country has two capitals and is home to the highest navigable lake in the world.

e. This country is home to the Incan ruins of Machu-Picchu and the oldest university in South America.

f. This country is bordered by Brazil, Argentina and Bolivia. It is also landlocked.

g. This country is the narrowest country in South America and is home to the statue of the Christ of the Andes.

h. This country is the richest oil-producing country and the northernmost country of South America.

i. This country exports bananas, cocoa, coffee, shrimp and petroleum. The Galapagos Islands are located off the coast of this country.

j. Three of these countries are located in the South Temperate Zone, meaning that their seasons are the reverse of ours.

| 82 / 102 |

Score _____

Teacher check _____
                            Initial   Date

VII. SPEAKING, WRITING AND READING PRACTICE

Let's Read

 Read the following passage and then respond to the questions after.

Mariana va de compras con su amiga, Pilar. Ellas quieren comprar la ropa nueva para el verano. Mariana quiere las sandalias y un traje de baño. Pilar prefiere mirar los pantalones cortos y las camisetas. Las dos van a la playa con sus familia. En la tienda Mariana no puede decidir en el traje de baño azul o el verde. Pilar dice que el azul parece más bonito. Entonces Mariana decidio comprar el verde. Pilar encuentra tres pantalones cortos—azules, blancos y negros. Decidio en los negros. Y también encuentra una camiseta amarilla, verde y negra. Decidio comprar la camiseta.

Después de comprar la ropa deciden ir al café. Mariana toma un sandwich de atún, papas fritas y un vaso de agua. Pilar toma una ensalada, pan y té frio. La comida es deliciosa. A Pilar le gusta la ensalada mucha. Tiene lechuga, tomates, huevos, queso, zanahorias, y la salsa de la casa. Las chicas hablan de su viaje. Van a nadar en el océano, jugar vólibol en la arena, observar a la gente, y por las noches van a jugar mini-golfo. También a las dos les gusta caminar por la playa. Les gusta sentirse la arena en los pies. Usualmente hay muchos jovenes allí. Les gusta hacer nuevos amigos. No pueden esperar el viaje.

7.1
1. Mariana y Pilar _____.
   a. compran los abrigo   b. compran la ropa de verano   c. necesitan sombreros

2. Mariana necesita algo para _____.
   a. trabajar   b. comer   c. nadar en el oceáno

3. Pilar compra _____.
   a. los pantalones cortos   b. las sandalias   c. un sandwich

4. Después de ir de compras las dos van _____.
   a. a casa   b. al café   c. a la playa

5. La comida es _____.
   a. deliciosa   b. bien   c. horrible

Let's Write

 Answer the following general questions in complete Spanish sentences.

7.2
a. ¿Qué ropa necesita para comenzar la escuela?

b. ¿Qué ropa necesita para ir a la playa?

c. ¿Qué ropa necesita para jugar en el invierno?

d. ¿Cuál es tu ropa favorita?

e. ¿Cuáles deportes prefieres jugar o mirar?

f. ¿Cuándo vienes a la escuela?

g. ¿Quién sabe lo más en la clase de español?

h. ¿Dónde prefieres estudiar?

i. ¿Por qué conoces a Madrid tan bueno?

j. ¿Qué tienen Uds. que hacer esta noche?

Let's Listen

Listen to the following passages and then respond to the questions after.

7.3   1. ¿Adónde van esta familia? _____
      a. a casa   b. a la tienda   c. al restaurante

      2. El hermanito tiene _____ .
      a. ensalada   b. hamburguesa con papas fritas   c. pizza

7.4   1. ¿Por qué Juana va al supermercado? _____
      a. para la comida   b. para las ropas   c. para las bebidas.

      2. ¿Qué va a comprar Juana? _____
      a. legumbres   b. frutas   c. los dos

7.5   1. ¿Qué estudia la clase? _____
      a. el cuerpo   b. nada   c. la comedia

      2. El pelo, la nariz, la boca, las ojos, las orejas son partes de _____ .
      a. la pierna   b. la cabeza   c. los brazos

Let's Speak

Create a conversation using the following cues.

7.6   You run into a friend and have a discussion.

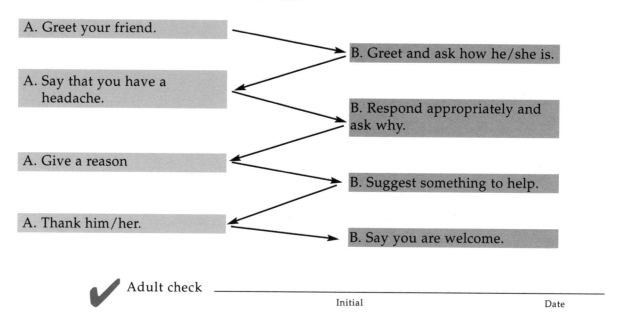

A. Greet your friend.

B. Greet and ask how he/she is.

A. Say that you have a headache.

B. Respond appropriately and ask why.

A. Give a reason

B. Suggest something to help.

A. Thank him/her.

B. Say you are welcome.

✔ Adult check _____

                               Initial   Date

7.7   You and a friend are practicing large numbers.

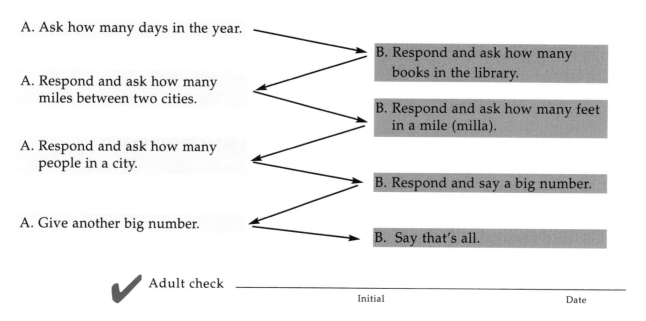

A. Ask how many days in the year.

B. Respond and ask how many books in the library.

A. Respond and ask how many miles between two cities.

B. Respond and ask how many feet in a mile (milla).

A. Respond and ask how many people in a city.

B. Respond and say a big number.

A. Give another big number.

B. Say that's all.

✔ Adult check _____

                               Initial   Date

Note: This section does not have a Self Test.

VIII. GRAMMAR REVIEW

Fill in the blank with the correct form of the verb in parentheses.

8.1

    a. Yo_____ los libros sobre la mesa. (poner)

    b. Luis_____ los libros en su cuarto. (poner)

    c. Yo_____ la tarea. (hacer)

    d. Nts. _____ el trabajo. (hacer)

    e. Yo_____ a las seis. (salir)

    f. Tú _____ las nueve y media. (salir)

    g. Yo_____ de la bicicleta. (caer)

    h. Ellos _____ de las bicicletas. (caer)

    i. Yo_____ las bebidas. (traer)

    j. Uds. _____ las frutas. (traer)

Fill in the blank with the correct form of the verb in parentheses.

8.2

    a. Yo_____ tres hermanos. (tener)

    b. Nts. _____ a la escuela a las ocho. (venir)

    c. Tú _____ decir la verdad. (poder)

    d. Uds. _____ las respuestas. (recordar)

    e. Yo_____ que sí. (pensar)

    f. Los chicos _____ el fútbol. (jugar)

    g. Tú _____ la puerta. (cerrar)

    h. Nts. _____ la lección. (entender)

    i. Yo_____ la camisa azul. (pedir)

    j. Ellas _____ la comida. (servir)

Decide whether saber **or** conocer **goes in the blank and write the correct form.**

8.3

    1. Yo_____ a Miguel bien.

    2. Nts. _____ jugar tenis.

    3. Uds. _____ la verdad.

    4. Tú _____ Madrid.

    5. Ella _____ el español.

Identify the clothing each person is wearing.

a. **b.** **c.** **d.** **e.**

8.4

a. _____

_____

b. _____

_____

c. _____

_____

d. _____

_____

e. _____

_____

Identify the lettered parts of the person.

8.5

a. _____

b. _____

c. _____

e. _____

f. _____

g. _____

h. _____

i. _____

j. _____

k. _____

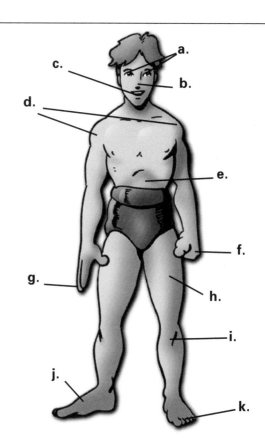

44

Answer the following questions in complete Spanish sentences.

8.6   1. ¿Qué te gusta jugar?

      2. ¿Dónde prefieres ir?

      3. ¿Quién va a salir a las diez?

      4. ¿Cuál es tu color favorito?

      5. ¿Cuándo tienes que estudiar?

 Fill in the blank with the correct possessive adjective that agrees with the subject.

8.7   1. Yo tengo _____ libros de escuela.

      2. Nts. visitamos a _____ abuelos.

      3. Tú pones_____ coche en el garaje.

      4. Ud. dice _____ respuesta.

      5. Ellos caen de_____ bicicletas.

Translate the following sentences to Spanish.

8.8   1. I like the red shirt.

      2. We like to read.

      3. Paul, you like to play.

      4. They like the shirts.

      5. He likes the cars.

Note: This section does not have a Self Test.

LIFEPAC 6: VOCABULARY LIST

El vocabulario de la comida – food vocabulary:

El desayuno	breakfast
El almuerzo	lunch
La cena	dinner
La merienda	snack

Las comidas:

la carne	meat
la carne asada	roast beef
el pollo	chicken
el pescado	fish
las chuletas de cerdo	pork chops
el biftec	steak
la ternera	veal
el jamón	ham
la hamburguesa	hamburger
el tocino	bacon

Los legumbres or las verduras – vegetables:

los frijoles	beans
las papas	potatoes
las zanahorias	carrots
las habichuelas	green beans
el maíz	corn
las espinacas	spinach
los guisantes	peas
la lechuga	lettuce
el tomate	tomato

Las frutas – fruits:

la manzana	apple
las uvas	grapes
las fresas	strawberries
la pera	pear
la naranja	orange
el melón	melon
el melocotón	peach
la piña	pineapple
el plátano	banana

Los postres – desserts:

los pasteles	pastries
las tartas	pies
el helado	ice cream
el pastel	cake
el flan	carmel custard

Las bebidas – drinks:

el agua	water
la leche	milk
el jugo	juice
el refresco	soft drink
el café	coffee
el té	tea
el chocolate	hot chocolate
el batido	shake

Otras comidas – other foods:

la sal	salt
la pimienta	pepper
el azúcar	sugar
la mantequilla	butter
el pan	bread
la mermelada	jam
la sopa	soup
las papas fritas	French fries
el cereal	cereal
los huevos	eggs
un sandwich	a sandwich
el yogur	yogurt
el arroz	rice
la pizza	pizza
la pasta	pasta

Verbs:

comer	to eat
tomar	to have, as in food or drink, to take
beber	to drink
preparar	to prepare
cocinar	to cook
pedir	to order
poner la mesa	to set the table
dar las gracias	to thank, give thanks, be thankful
dar un paseo	to take a walk
dar a	to face
ver	to see
agradecer	to thank (yo agradezco)
aparecer	to appear (yo aparezco)
conducir	to drive, conduct (yo conduzco)
desaparecer	to disappear (yo desaparezco)
obedecer	to obey (yo obedezco)
ofrecer	to offer (yo ofrezco)
parecer	to seem, look like (yo parezco)
producir	to produce (yo produzco)
reconocer	to recognize (yo reconozco)
traducir	to translate (yo traduzco)

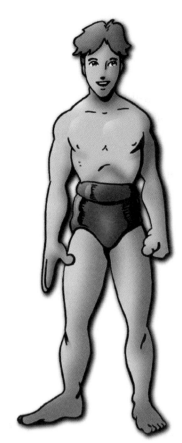

El cuerpo humano – the human body:

la cabeza	the head
el pelo	the hair
los ojos	the eyes
la nariz	the nose
las orejas, los oídos	the ears
la boca	the mouth
el diente	the tooth
el cuello	the neck
el hombro	the shoulders
el brazo	the arm
la mano	the hand
los dedos	the fingers
el estómago	the stomach
la espalda	the back
la pierna	the leg
la rodilla	the knee
el pie	the foot
los dedos del pie	the toes

Idioms:

tener dolor de	to have an ache
doler	to hurt, to ache
Hacer una pregunta	to ask a question
Hacer un viaje	to take a trip.
Hacer la maleta	to pack a
	suitcase
Haga Ud. el favor	
de + an infinitive	please
echar de menos	to miss
echar una carta al correo	to mail a letter
creer que sí (no)	to think so (not)
estar de pie	to be standing
querer decir	to mean
salir bien (mal)	to come out well
	(badly), to pass
	(fail)

Numbers:

100 – 900

100	ciento (cien)
200	doscientos, as
300	trescientos, as
400	cuatrocientos, as
500	quinientos, as
600	seiscientos, as
700	setecientos, as
800	ochocientos, as
900	novecientos, as

1,000 – 100,000,000

1,000	mil
5,000	cinco mil
100,000	cien mil
1,000,000	millón (de)
5,000,000	cinco millones (de)
100,000,000	cien millones (de)

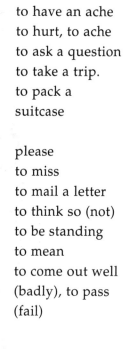